Valentina Mezcalito Blues

Catfish McDaris

First edition

ISBN: 978-1-7371509-7-8

published by Laughing Ronin Press 2021

cover art by Jeff Filipski

Table of Contents

Valentina Mezcalito Blues

Humanity Matters

Sixty-eight years ago, on Route 66
I was born near the Sangre de Cristos

Yesterday the love of my life and I
saw a protest sign that read: Save A

Life, Kill A Cop, my Mexican wife cried,
my knuckles clenched the steering wheel

Our young daughter is a rookie cop, in
the bloody torn streets of Milwaukee

Black Hawk helicopters patrol the skies,
army snipers are assigned to the roofs

Of all the police stations, rioters are
throwing Molotov cocktails, bricks,

And bullets, they loot stores and burn
neighborhoods and aggravate the pandemic

I cleaned my weapons, I hadn't touched

for forty years, anybody wants to hurt

Our blue angel will pay, I will take war

unto thy streets, until my guns fall lifeless.

The Night Jimi Hendrix Asked Me to Dance

When you fall in love, you lose all five of your senses. Oscar Chavez

Valentina and Dancer hadn't been
together long, after a heated discussion
with friends, about great bands

Moby Grape, Strawberry Alarm Clock,
Spooky Tooth, Iron Butterfly, Buffalo
Springfield, they all went to a dance

Three couples hit the floor, crazy wild
uninhibited throwing hair and hips, after
five fast songs, they played John Lennon's

My Girl, Valentina tried to lead, Dancer
frowned, she said, "You dance like a
cowboy," "That's my Texas Two-Step."

"We need practice," they all sat down for

a breather, Mendes and John drank a beer,

a young black dude asked Dancer to dance

Dancer said, "No thanks, I've never danced

with a man," "That's not what you told me

last week. We spent the night dancing

Together. You told me I looked just like

your hero, Jimi Hendrix," Almost everyone

at the table was laughing and crying.

Oh Baby Baby

Valentina had a perverted sense
of humor and a wild imagination

That was one of the many reasons
Dancer was totally in love with her

Valentina's sister, Rosita was seven
years older and barely missed being

An old maid, she married a cowboy
looking dude that had been married

Five times and loved to sniff out loose
ladies, he made wine, croquet sets, chess

Boards, metal Civil War men, he was an
interesting guy, but had a wandering eye

Rosita quit a job in Mexico as a bank
manager and moved to Chicago, with

No English, Dancer got bad vibes from the
situation, after two years her cowpoke quit his

Teaching job and moved to St. Paul to sell
hearing aids to pig farmers, Rosita spoke

English by then and refused to return to
Mexico, she was at Valentina's house every

Day, Dancer said this had to stop, Valentina
agreed, she made a meal of mystery meat

Rosita grabbed a tortilla full and took a big,
bite, she spit it all over the table and even

Globs slid down the wall, she said, "What the
hell is that?" Valentina said, "Baby meat."

"Baby meat?" "Yes, baby meat, it's nice and
tender and full of vitamin B," Dancer said,

"The hospitals have plenty and they're cheap,"
Rosita packed her suitcase, bound for Tabasco.

Three Red Horses Rice

Was long grained rice was from Thailand,
Dancer watched in amazement at how fast
Valentina ate with chopsticks, while he tried
to keep up with a fork, she smelled of Blue
Lizard Sunscreen from Australia, it was

Tantalizing, Valentia laughed at what her
girlfriend had told her, that she'd seen Dancer
with a pretty black lady that resembled Aunt
Jemima, Valentina told her his doctor had

Prescribed a black woman a week for his
asthma, Dancer loved her so much, at times
he felt like he was hanging on by his teeth and
fingernails, as the world spun out of control.

Komodo Dragon Tongue

Pablito never cared much for eating pussy, saying it was like eating tuna through a picket fence. He complained of chapped lips, tired tongue, lock jaw, bushy eyebrows and mustache, and stretched out ears like tortillas. All Pablo craved was the missionary position with an occasional back door approach, but alas his reputation as a cunt gobbler preceded him. I told him repeatedly that he was the junkyard dog of poontang. He'd tilt his head back, grin and howl like a werewolf with hemorrhoids, revealing pubic hair caught between his teeth. "I need to get out of this hole I've dug."

"Why don't you try bullfighting or spelunking or ornithology or become a Caliban?" I suggested. He packed a bag, got his record albums, and boogied. The doorbell rang, it was a dishwater blonde in a tight canary yellow dress, polka dot stiletto hills, and French fish net stockings. I rotated my neck muscles, stretched my tongue Komodo dragon fashion, and opened the door. The last vestiges of the sun were a dropping guillotine, and an evil pumpkin moon was sneering down.

Monte Alban

Valentina was unusual, she had it all. When she whistled, Dancer sat up and begged. Dancer did a few minor masonry jobs, shot a mean game of snooker, and was a professional expert harmless Dancer. Valentina taught Spanish. They lived in a shotgun flat temporarily. Dancer said their landlady was like the old chick that kept a fart in her shoe. They planned a trip south of the border to visit, Carlotta and Benito. They were Valentina's parents and lived just outside of Mexico City. Dancer knew the Aztec story of the warrior, Popcatepti, who was promised the princess, Iztaccihuati's hand in marriage. Then her father did not keep his word and they both died of broken hearts. Their bodies became mountains overlooking Mexico City. The sky was lumpy cloud gray gravy as they rode the train. They listened to Death Cab for A Cutie and music from the Andes. Carlotta enjoyed stories and jokes, Benito smoked Cuban cigars and played dominoes. Valentina slept in a north bedroom, Dancer thought they'd put him next to the chicken house. He wanted to strangle a rooster every fucking sleepless morning.

Carlotta told a story about bricklayers digging the foundation for their house and finding some old human bones. Carlotta consulted with Benito, and they told them to take the bones to the church. The church told the men to take them to the Federales. They sent the bones back where they were dug up. They made a grave away from the house. Their neighbor Guillermo was a matador from Spain that had lost his nerve. He was a good friend of the family. A lady at the Mercado promised to give Carlotta an avocado tree, so she had her sons dig a hole for it. Guillermo lived a block away and would take a shortcut through their backyards. One night he stepped in the hole for the tree, and he started screaming, "The dead man has me by my leg. Help. Help." Everyone went outside to save Guillermo. When he got home, he saw his cat was outside on the porch. He grabbed it and took it inside, only to discover he had an extremely mad skunk. Benito smelled something and heard a knocking at the door, it was Guillermo wanting to watch the bullfights on television. Carlotta pulled the door curtain aside and wagged her finger no.

Valentina and Dancer hiked to a valley where vanilla, coffee, and cinnamon grew. Building a warm fire under the hypnotic stars, they fell into a deep sleep. Waking Dancer looked for Valentina, but there was no sign of her. He returned to where her parent's house was, it had vanished like it never existed. There was an avocado tree with a pinata of Valentina smiling from Monte Alban. He hit it with a thick stick, a map and love poem floated out. Dancer walked slowly down the mountain. He came to an adobe cantina surrounded by goats. There was an old man playing solitaire, Dancer ordered a cerveza and asked about his friends. The barmaid had a big ugly wart, which made Dancer ill. He went outside, and an old man was shuffling cards. The cards were completely white on both sides. A goat butted his elbow, spilling his beer. He figured it was time to wander south until he found the pyramid with Valentina waiting for him.

Swordfish Trombone

I see ears in the swirling starry night.
the sky is drunk, the sun puking lemon
juice, the moon has a toothache, the lady
asked the dope fiend to come to talk to
Jesus, he stinks of absinthe and funk.

Sometimes at night I meet
myself when I was young,
I disgust myself now

What color is the wind?
What color is an orgasm?
What color is death?

There is no sea of tranquility
There's no such thing as a small miracle

Drinking Mexican coffee as black as death
Lady Gaga drives up in a dirty Mercury,
they head to the Valley of Rhinoceroses

Listening to Swordfish Trombone and
Bitches Brew overlooking Mexico City.

A Can of DEATH

The snow melted upon her skin
hot drifting desert sand blown
smooth hungry and beautiful

The two wars inside each person
go on forever, love and hate
the sky always a gun barrel blue gray

After she left all was loneliness and
one can on a table the label read
DEATH, eat it before it eats you.

Her Taco Tasted Like Rain

Our love making was like a spaghetti
western; good, bad, and ugly

Her freckles were devil's kisses
showering down from purgatory

She used to striptease, while a monkey
played viola and the organ grinder did just that

Stumbling through time, I wished I'd never
eaten her shit sandwich lies

She drove stakes through my
obsidian oblivious soul

Slipping and melting through my fingers
like mawkish snow and raging wind.

My cheeks were wet rivers,
tears swimming from Nagasaki

My heart imploded and exploded

in the fiery pain of Hiroshima

Blood in the salt, lime, and tequila

I know now I should've cared more for you.

Gallup, New Mexico

Dancer had lots of stories about women he'd been with. Many were odd, but this one blew his mind. He spoke of when he'd met Valentina at a powwow in Gallup. Her beauty took his breath away, it made his legs grow weak, and she was indescribable. It was lust at first sight for both of them.

They shacked up in a motel on Route 66 for a week, then traveled south along the Gila River camping until they hit Geronimo's raiding grounds. Valentina said she was a relative of Geronimo from the Bedonkohe Chiricahua Apache. Dancer told her he was related to Wilma Mankiller of the Panther Clan of the Cherokee.

They settled at a hot spring where the Apaches would rest after raiding into Mexico. It was surrounded by peyote cacti and datura. Valentina made a potion for Dancer and her to shapeshift and to dream and seek visions. It contained Lophophora williamsii peyote, moonflower jimsonweed datura, yerba buena, yucca flowers, and mesquite beans made into pinole.

Dancer dreamed of a warrior sitting atop Mount Rushmore first offering sage to the four directions and chanting. The warrior moved over to sit on each president, and he filled his long ceremonial pipe as he smoked, his body became enveloped in a turquoise cloud. He chanted four times and the mountain carvings crumbled into sand. The warrior did this to all four presidents until they disappeared.

Then a huge cloud formed over the clean mountain in it was a herd of buffalo with mounted warriors chasing them. He ran and vaulted bareback onto spotted horse, and they galloped toward the horizon.

Dancer woke up hearing the sounds of hooves running like thunder in the sky. In the sand were perfect images of George Washington, Thomas Jefferson, Theodore Roosevelt, and Abraham Lincoln.

He was alone except for a tarantula, a scorpion, and a rattlesnake, and a roadrunner looking at him, like he better hit the road.

Christmas Chunky Man Soup

Find turtles, hit them with a fucking sledgehammer
you'll get seven flavors: pork, chicken, beef, shrimp,
veal, fish, or goat I ate with three Chinese funeral
strippers they could give a dead man a hard on

Some people eat meat but can't kill it or process it
this makes less sense, than either the content meat
eaters or the moral vegetarians, after the trains ran in
China the donkeys weren't needed, so they·ate them

Cats in Thailand, dogs by the Apache, horses in France,
a six-hundred-pound octopus can shrink itself down to
fit through the size of a quarter, then expand, carrots
and potatoes scream when you rip them up, just because
we don't understand their language, means nothing

The strippers suggested we eat death row and lifer inmates
due to overpopulation and the money, we waste on them
there should be a way to skin and humanely slaughter them
and make them fit for consumption like chunky man soup.

Dolly Parton and Vincent van Gogh

Dancer gets hit by Dolly Parton's tour bus. He passes out and wakes up in her bed, they knock off a good romp and she puts on a movie with Willem Dafoe playing van Gogh. Dancer tells Dolly it's bullshit, Vincent looks like he just stepped out of a barber shop in every scene. She and Dancer go around and around, then he asks her to play Jolene, she says she'll have to put on a t-shirt because her titties are so big, she can't get to her guitar. She removes the shirt after the song and Dancer woke up on a park bench wearing that shirt with her perfume. He hears, Tom Waits singing Christmas Card from a Hooker in Minneapolis.

And Her Eyes Made Love to Him

They ran barefoot through the yucca,
prickly pear, goat head stickers, and
mesquite like a monster was after them

Dancer told her he loved her, his heart
was destroyed, limping away, she shot
him the finger, he wondered if it was

His intelligence quotient or hers, she
was pissed, earlier they'd been shopping
for new panties for her and an umbrella

A six-year-old boy was with his attractive
mother, they walked by a well endowed
mannequin in an aquatic avocado bikini

He jerked the bottom of the suit to the
floor, Dancer cracked up laughing and
blurted out, "Way to go, little man."

He grabbed the half-dressed dummy and
sprinted from the store, a fat security
guard gave chase, Valentina and Dancer

Lost their sandals, he circled back for
their El Camino, the cops were waiting
with steel bracelets, he hoped it would

Be for a short visit and his lady would
have pity and go his bail, and let him
pay for and keep his newest amiga.

Put My Burning Blood in Your Alligator Purse

Manipulated, stimulated, mutilated
spindled, swindled, brindled, kindled
castigated, masticated, I'm on fire

Trump says we'll travel seventeen
times faster now than ever before, his
caps read Making America Great Again

I wear a mask, I don't want to be careful
I want to be dangerous, who is stealing
all my grocery money, you have to rob

A bank to buy a hamburger, I eat Son Of
A Bitch Stew every damned night and wait
on an armed response, it's all a cacophony

You can't see love, but it still exists, don't
cry, the piano sounds like a toaster, jumping
in the sink while you're washing dishes.

Damn Good Cheese

Dancer just finished smoking
some good cheese and sipping
Thunderbird, he was almost
finished reading LeRoi Jones'

Preface to a Twenty Volume
Suicide Note, Amiri Baraka had
signed it for him, he heard a tap
at the door, it was one of his gal

Pals, she wanted to watch TV and
get laid, she took a shower and
came out in a white silk negligee,
Dancer said, "I don't know what

To do first, lick you or dick you,"
"Take your pick Slick," She turned
on NYPD Blue, "How come those

dudes can piss without holding their
Peckers?" Dancer just shrugged,

he wrote: You got me on fire baby
like parakeets in Marrakesh I've
been in the doghouse all my life

Bad people come in all flavors from
Placitas, Tijeras Canyon, Jemez Hot
Springs, Tucumcari, Raton, Santa Fe,
she pressed against him, they smiled.

Amigos Siempre

Dancer sat on the dock smoking
a cig he'd rolled, he thought about
how expensive tobacco was now,
killing yourself ought to be cheaper

He waited on trucks to arrive, so
they could be unloaded and maybe
he could catch a catnap in the sun

Dancer's strongman Frank loomed,
putting him in the shadows, "You've
met my Uncle Big Nate, he's starting
a roofing business on the Northside.
Can you think of any catchy names?"

"How about: Niggers With Big Ham-
mers? It will draw attention, both black
and white. You could draw some soul
brothers with big hammers for business

cards, stationary, t-shirts, and logos for trucks. Nate will clean up big time."

"You are one crazy motherfucker."
"I know, but that's why we're amigos."

Picasso Strip

Jerzy slowly inched off her chartreuse crotch less panties with a striptease magic flair. Jose was harder than howitzer cannons, he fired during his stint in the army. Her perfectly coiffed pussy almost had a hypnotic mind of its own. She danced and swirled around the room. Jose had on the television, but he couldn't pay attention. There was an important breaking news bulletin. Jose craned his neck to see what had happened. There was smoke, fire, screaming people, police, firetrucks, and ambulances. Jerzy had her sequined bra and spider webbed nylons off and twirling over her head. She slung them against the wall, and they hung on top of their copy of Pablo Picasso's Reclining Nude painted in 1932.

Walter Cronkite spoke of a government building being blown up by a fertilizer bomb. It was too early in the rescue attempts to determine the death toll. Then a commercial came on about douche products and peanut butter.

Jose pinned Jerzy to the couch and made her squeal and screech. Jerzy was in heaven, with her smoothly shaved legs wrapped around Jose's waist. He picked her up, not missing a stroke, and retrieved two ice cold bottles of Miller High Life.

They watched the tragedy unfold. 19 children, 3 unborn babies, and 149 adults died in Oklahoma City in April of 1995. Blood and tears filled the land. They finished their beers and kept on fucking.

Fools in an Inferno

Squeeze my lemons 'til the juice runs down my legs. Robert Johnson
1937

The elephant tusk colored guitar was like a 1954 Jaguar XK120M being revved and coiled, in a brake stand of anticipation. Lightning fingers departed on a riff, stepping off the brake pedal, stomping the gas. The brains and minds were blown into a liver looking oil smudge cloud. All thoughts were vaporized and flung toward the rings of Saturn.

Reaching into a tattered guitar case, adorned with a Grateful Dead skeleton, the Viking looking musician retrieved a violin bow. Twirling it like a magic wand, he applied it to his axe. He treated his instrument like a beautiful neurotic nymphomaniac, fondling, coaxing, and whispering to her with an evil mysterious grin. The ivory Hendrix Woodstock Stratocaster emitted an orgasmic cacophony of notes. The music built in layers of sounds and rhythms. It was an unearthly experience.

Dancer looked around to see if the other people were as affected as he was. Everyone's mouth was slightly ajar and drooling. A Rastafarian passed him a spleef, the size of a Fidel Castro special. Dancer didn't want to become distracted, so he handed it off. Some people were taking deep tokes, he needed nothing to intensify his musical nirvana. Looking around, Dancer saws lots of hair standing on end, even the Rasta man's dreadlocks were doing the hootchie cootchie.

A whimsical Gypsy lady bass player took over the lead. She hit chords and notes so low they rattled the walls, ceiling, bottles behind the bar, and every one's guts. When she unstrapped her

Rickenbacker 325 Capri, identical to John Lennon's he played on The Ed Sullivan Show and swiveled it around like a phallic extension, the audience froze. The guitar had been restrung as a bass like Jaco Pastorius played.

Her fingers bounced and plucked and strummed, swarms of sounds engulfed the room. She did the splits and ran the Rick over her amps. Feedback and reverberation screamed, moaned, and crackled through the blue electrified atmosphere. Spinal backbones felt as if they were being sliced into piles of bone chunks with meat cleavers and dull machetes. The bass was a hysterical chainsaw grinding the audience into a hypnotic state of awe raw meat.

Somebody said the drummer used to play with Iron Butterfly. A sparkling diamond serpentine pearl set of Gretsch drums surrounded and engulfed the Mongolian warrior man. A gigantic Asian gong glittered and glimmered in the background. Painted on one of the bass drums were the band members dressed as ancient Druids dancing around an erupting volcano. Fools was spelled out on the other drum. Starting his solo on two fur wrapped congas, a simple hip hop beat, soon his hands were a blur of speed. He became invisible and a complicated rhythm emerged. Soon his legs were pounding like pistons, the noise level was a deafening thunderous assault on the ears. Next his telephone pole sized arms were all over the kit in a whirling dervish tornado assault. He slowed to strip off his soaked sweatshirt, exposing exquisite tattoos over his entire upper torso. Warrior man ended his barrage with a machinegun assault on the gong, like he was trying to wake all the dead emperors in China.

A cloud of smoke engulfed the stage and a monstrous fire breathing dragon blew out a tremendous ball of flames. An eerie voice laughed and said, "We'll be back in fifteen with something you can dance to." The band disappeared in a turquoise haze.

The people staggered and swooned in ecstasy. Everyone went outside to look at the stars. The wind blew through the aspens and spruce trees. The stream stones spoke to the water that bathed them. There was a brass spittoon on the stage filled with glowing red embers. The band had vanished with their instruments and equipment. The bartender acted baffled.

Romeo Fever

It was too early for a beer, Romeo decided to study a few art history books about the female nudes, he loved to paint. The librarian looked exceptionally ravishing; she resembled Marilyn Monroe with the blue-black hair of Cleopatra. She had book worm intelligence about her, what you might expect in a small village library. There was Mona Lisa laughter dancing behind her flirtatious radiant eyes. Her hair had a few strands of gray and her glasses gave her a studious appeal. Romeo's dark wavy hair, green blue intense penetrating eyes, sensuous smile, and slim muscular body usually had a positive effect on women. He asked her about books of beautiful naked women painted by Egon Schiele, Gustave Courbet, and Paul Gauguin. Romeo explained his desire to capture the face of a lady in the throes of an orgasm. He could tell this piqued her interest as she directed him to a small secluded area, where the books were located. It was unusually silent; he could hear a clock ticking on the wall. There was no one besides himself and the librarian in the building. The books he wanted were on the top shelves and out of reach. At the end of the aisle was a ladder with wheels connected to a rail, along the top and bottom of the bookcase. A sign on the wall read, For Librarian's Use Only. Romeo walked back to the desk to ask for assistance. The librarian was turned away from the counter, working bent over a stack of books. He checked out her figure. Her body was outstanding and extremely desirable. He could feel his member growing stiff as he cleared his throat to get her attention. 'Excuse me, Miss, I need you,' he said. She turned and raised an eyebrow in inquiry. 'There's a book I can't quite reach,' Romeo explained. She followed him without a word, back to the aisle in question. He pointed to the books he required. She slid the ladder down the rail and brushed against Romeo's huge growing erection, as she started up the ladder. She had long smooth legs, ending in black lacy panties. As she started back down, he ran one hand up the back of her thigh and with the other rubbed her wet pussy, massaging her clitoris and inserting a finger. She stopped above him on the last rung of the ladder and made a low purring cat like sound in the back of her throat. He rolled her panties down off one leg and she kicked them out of the way. Romeo lifted her skirt and cupped both cheeks of her ass, spreading her open. He put his tongue inside her vagina and teased and nibbled her clitoris, as she hunched him like there was no tomorrow. 'Not here, please, please, please, goddamn you,' she moaned. In the next breath she kept saying, 'Yes, yes, fuck yes,' over and over. She pulled Romeo's face into her drenched feverish pussy. Romeo dropped his pants and slowly lowered her down off the ladder on to his humongous throbbing penis. He impaled her and thrust for all he was worth, working in and out. Plunging left and right, deep and shallow, working like a maniac stallion jackhammer, he almost pulled all the way out, until she screamed for more. He removed her shirt and bra; Romeo's tongue and mouth tantalized her perfect breasts and beautiful nipples. She became almost uncontrollable; her hair came undone and grew wilder by the second. Books and shelves rattled with a frenzied earthquake rhythm. So far, they hadn't been discovered. The librarian's eyes glazed over in pleasure and passion, but there was also a hint of terror. Romeo locked this face in his memory for a painting later as they finished, in a nearly collapsing mutual orgasm. Feeling a bit worn out, but far from entirely satiated, they fixed their clothes and he left to get his oil paints and canvas. The librarian decided to close the library early for her appointment to pose for Romeo.

Unbridled lust engulfed her mind, body, and soul like a mountain torrential rainstorm sending walls of water down the dry arroyos of the desert. Her thighs and nipples trembled and throbbed as she thought of her ex-lover Dancer.

Red Bird Peppers

When we got to central Mexico,
the universe changed into magic
Valentina's Uncle Beto picked

Up Dancer and Val at the train station
in Mexico City after a long trip across
Chihuahua, his old Chevy was held

Together with bailing wire and duct tape
they were headed to a valley where coffee
and cinnamon grew, soon they were

Climbing higher into the mountains, snow
covered peaks could be seen off in the
distance as well as smoke from an active

Volcano, two young laughing lads jumped in
the back seat, one had a pig under his arm
the other had a chicken and they were

Having a shitting contest, Valentina introduced

her nephews to Dancer, they soon arrived

at their casa, Tia Lupita was all smiles

Dancer gave her some cheese from Northern

Italy, she made soup with the rind and threw

in a handful of tiny red bird peppers

They washed naked in the stream and were

soon asleep, Dancer dreamed of making dream

catchers with Navajo friends in New Mexico.

A Bad Day

Ms. Convenient Fuck #1 left

an anatomically correct

inflatable woman on my porch

I watched a ladybug crawl into

the round orifice between its legs

Ms. Convenient Fuck #2 mailed

Me a dirty magazine, a jar of

petroleum jelly, and a box of tissues

Ms. Convenient Fuck #3 arrived

Two hours later for dinner, with

hickeys up and down her neck, she

proclaimed her love for #1 and #2

I decided to squash the ladybug.

Pelicano Boogie

"Two degrees in bebop, a PhD in swing, he's a master of rhythm, a rock 'n' roll king." Lowell George of Little Feat

A buttery sun painted the walls red
her fingers shadowed the tune

Ran circles all around the ivories
her bullfrog bass never hitting on the nose

Notes traveling high messages in the sky
loop de loop an inverted Jenny bringing it home

When the quiet grew the light faded to black
the pelicans bopped with the fishes in their beaks.

Getting Lucky

Jose, Dancer's primo sat in the kitchen
reading his taco sauce splattered copy
of a Bukowski, he was pissed off, be-
cause his sister, Pilar was running with

Some low riders, getting up he washed
his dishes and went to the bathroom and
checked the Virgin of Guadalupe tattoo
in the mirror, it was itchy, but looked good

Pilar's bra hung from the shower rod, he
tried it on and smiled, she had big tits,
Jose had just finished a nickel in college,
for grand theft auto, with a kilo of grass

He took off the bra and threw it out the
window, the phone rang, but he didn't
answer, figuring it was for Pilar, the door
bell rang, he ignored that too, lying on the

Couch, he studied the ceiling, Pilar had
painted a mural of the life of Frida Kahlo,
she had talent, looks, and intelligence, but
he doubted if she would escape the barrio

Jose heard gunshots outside the window, he
investigated, two soul brothers were bleeding
heavily on the sidewalk, fuck it he thought
closing the curtains, he listened to the sirens

And drifted off to sleep, dreaming of Dancer
getting lucky with his gorgeous schoolteacher.

My Grandma Ate Boogers

My uncle gave me a farm cat,
he was pretty cool mostly, but
would scratch up the furniture
and meow loud at night

I named him Boogers because
my sister always had her finger
up her nose and wiped her boogers
on the walls, Boogers liked to
lick them off for a snack

He always took care of his
business outside, slept with
me, but he'd drag in dead
birds or mice making mama mad

Then Boogers gave me the fleas,
I came home from school itching,
Booger wasn't around anywhere

I asked mama where was Boogers,

she said he went to live with your
grandparents in the nursing home,
I got a real bad feeling about that.

Yellow in Spanish

My brother called from a
town outside of Tulsa, he
needed my help to remove
some unsavory characters

He knew I'd been in almost
up to my neck in Vietnam and
most of my life, he referred
to me as an overachiever

It felt kind of strange wearing
a star, since I'd always walked
in shadows of good and wicked

My first day on the job, I met
a thief, rapist, and child abuser
all rolled into one, I gave him
fair warning, he pulled his pistol

His hog leg barrel traveled straight

toward me, I double tapped his chest,

his lungs splattered the wall

He was dead an instant before his legs

received the message, finally he folded

like a house of cards, he made a sound

like a broken sick accordion bagpipe

I stayed for a week, I didn't have to kill

anybody else, my brother was relieved

when I laid my badge on his desk,

everyone was resting a lot easier

Pointing my Ford west, I headed for

Amarillo and a senorita that could make

enchiladas so good, they'd bring tears

to your eyes and a smile to your belly.

Boom Motherfucker

My daughter met a guy, a young
parole officer that teaches hand
gun marksmanship to the entire
Milwaukee Police Force, he told

Us about a lady supervisor that
accidentally fired into the ceiling,
after he'd called for a cease fire

"She left one in the pipe, anybody
injured?" I asked, he shook his head,
no "Was she canned?" again, no

"We had a guy in boot camp drop a
grenade, the drill sergeant kicked it
down a hole and almost got his foot
blown off" he asked, "What happened?"

"They gave him another chance, sort
of, he had to lie on his back with his

56

feet running in the air, pumping his
weapon up and down and repeating

'I am a dying cockroach' for what
to his sorry ass seemed like the rest
of his life or maybe he dreamed of
becoming Kafka's Metamorphosis

He dropped a potato masher and the
sergeant got his combat boot with foot
inside, blown sky high, his ankle looked
like worms having bloody sex.

Howitzers in Paris

A lady from Paris wanted to be friends on Face Book, I thought why not. She sent me some poems and art for a blog I have with a lady poet partner. We posted her poems and some of the art. Her drawings were sort of Kama Sutra style. Awhile later she wrote and announced she had a book for sale about women that survived cancer. I'm always glad to hear of people conquering their diseases. I wrote and congratulated her on beating cancer and wished her much success with her book. She wrote back that she'd never had cancer, just that there were no books out on the subject. I asked my wife about this, and she laughed and Googled up hundreds of books about cancer. She was always telling me about how people would write books like they were experts about any damn thing. I'm sure she was hinting about my book from my artillery days in the army.

The Cell of Jeffrey Dahmer

Valentina inherited a house complete with furniture and a car in Milwaukee. She asked Dancer to go with her to settle her Aunt Betty's estate. They traveled by train from El Paso, the scenery was spectacular. Dancer had been a writer for a while, without much success. In his notes, he'd written: Crying on a balcony in Chicago…Superman never had to take a shit…The tamale had no meat, only a chicken bone…He was called Fart Face because his nose was always wrinkled in a grimace, The nun with the Frida Kahlo eyebrows, Driving with a ghetto lean. Valentina looked at his journal and asked, "What the fuck does any of this mean?"

They took train north to Milwaukee from Chicago. Valentina called Betty's lawyer and arranged a meeting for the next day. There was the Iron Horse Hotel close to the Harley Davidson Museum. They took a taxi there and showered, ate, and went to see Elvis Presley's Harley and all the choppers and hogs. Dancer noticed they were right next to the Wisconsin River and there was a moving coyote scaring away the seagulls from Lake Michigan. He asked about it, a museum worker said it was robotic and moved, to try to keep bird droppings off the cars and hogs.

The lawyer arranged a real estate broker to sell the house and furniture and he had a car dealership to take care of the car. Valentina agreed, but Dancer suggested they stay a few nights in the house and check things out. The lawyer wasn't pleased but gave them the keys to everything.

"You have to be difficult."

Dancer said, "I just want to make certain what you have before you sign on the dotted line. We don't that lawyer and most of them are weasels."

The taxi took them to a nice brick home neighborhood. Aunt Betty's house was two stories, red brick, with maple trees, and yews in the front. The backyard had fruit trees, grape vines, currants, perennial flowers, herbs, and blackberries. A key opened the detached two car garage, it held a Toyota Camry, a snow blower and lawn mower. The house had a safe and regulation sized pool table in the basement. Dancer told Valentina they needed to explore all of Betty's house before letting the lawyer get his greedy fingers on anything.

Dancer called his cousin in Veracruz about the safe. Tommy said, "Get me the dimensions, all the written information, and go buy a stethoscope, so I can listen to the tumblers over the phone."

"It's Hall Brothers safe, built in 1903, from Cincinnati, it is four and a half feet tall by three and a half feet wide. I got the best stethoscope on the market. Has anyone ever cracked a safe by phone?" Dancer said.

"This might be a first, Primo. It can be done. Let's proceed, put the scope just above the dial on the safe and put the earphones directly on the phone microphone." It took three tries, before the safe opened its mouth wide. Tommy asked, "Was there any treasure?"

"You wouldn't believe what's in there. Two padded envelopes of diamonds and over $320,000. You'll get a nice chunk of cheese, my brother. Once this northern adventure is over, we'll be back down south of the Rio Bravo."

Valentina and Dancer opened a bank account and rented a large safety deposit box for their new acquisitions. They kept their hotel and drove Betty's car; it was almost new with under 1,000 miles on it. They called several real estate agents for different opinions on their house and the current market.

The next-door neighbor had been checking them out. Valentina spoke to her over the short backyard fence. The lady was way too friendly too fast. She asked lots of questions and wanted to share her life story. They drifted toward the front yards. Valentina loved the pencil thin purple Siberian irises and asked Dancer to pick her a huge bouquet. He had his blade out and this barking slobbering brown dog lunged at him almost coming over the fence. Dancer had dog spit all over his face, he grabbed the dog's jaws and held them together. The neighbor yelled, "Eva, bad dog. Get your ass over here." She looked at Dancer in wonder, "I've never seen anyone stop a dog like that."

"I love dogs and all animals," Dancer said. "Her name is Eva?"

"Yes, Eva Braun, just like Hitler's woman. I name my kids and pets after The Beatles mostly, but this dog is a retard, so I use Nazi 's handles too."

Dancer excused himself to clean up. He thought, there was something not right with that woman. When Valentina didn't come inside, he looked out the window and saw she was still getting her ear bent and was looking around for an escape route. Dancer went outside and mimicked she had a phone call.

The neighbor said, "My name is Rosy, but folks call me Gypsy because I'm a burlesque dancer. This is my daughter, Lucy In The Sky, my son, Rocky Raccoon, and my other son, Maxwell the Human Silver Hammer and my daughter, Sexy Sadie. We call him the Human because we had a Maxwell the Dog, until Lucy killed her. She mixed Mr. Clean, Alpo, Play Doh, peanut butter, and tobacco and killed Max dead as hell."

"I got busted at this strip club I was working at, for giving lap dances completely naked. I had men trying to bone me twenty times a night. You're supposed to keep on at least a G-string. I rubbed my poontang all over them mofos and got the biggest tips." She laughed, "If you know what I mean? If you care for a private dance, I'm sure we could sneak one in?"

"I'm good for now, Gypsy." Dancer was easing away back into the house.

"You didn't let me finish my story about going to jail. The cops were real assholes. They threw me in the cell where they had caged Jeffrey Dahmer. Since then, all kinds of weird shit has been happening to me. Such as Lucy killing Maxwell the Dog. I was dating this asshat, I called Henry the Horse, and he got drunk and high and grabs a burlap bag and snatches two cats off a front porch. Henry slings them over his shoulder and keeps walking. Two blocks later, he retrieves one cat from the bag and starts eating it. He started at the back thigh and the cat is meowing and squirming, trying to get away. Henry bites into the cat's stomach and guts and heart. Blood is all over both of them, but the cat is silent. People are looking at them in disgust and shock. The bag over his shoulder is wiggling and bouncing. Henry is spitting out fur and bones. People are calling nine eleven and making movies of the ghastly horror. The police arrive before the Horse can begin eating the second cat. He did not go gently into the night. The cops lit him up real good with electricity. Then I hooked up with this Bungalow Bill dude, he watched porno and jacked off in all my shoes. I hit him in the dick with a rolling pin, repeatedly. His dick was limper than an over cooked lasagna noodle."

Clouds of Jeffrey Dahmer curse the entire city, especially where he was incarcerated. Dancer talked to Valentina. He suggested using their new lawyer, real estate agent and have them sell the car and household items and have the proceeds forwarded to her. They picked up the treasure from the safe and caught a flight to Oaxaca, Mexico.

Dancing With Comets

Xihuitl meant Dancing With Comets, his mother, Yaotli was Tarahumara Aztec. She gave him his name. His father wanted to call him Porterhouse after his favorite cut of meat. His mom insisted, he be called Dancer. Johnny, his dad was a brick mechanic, he could make brick, block, or stone come alive in a wall. Dancer naturally carried hod for him, mortar and whatever his dad was laying, setting up scaffolding, keeping the mortar mixer running, the water barrel full, the mortar boards wet, and the mortar stirred to the perfect consistency. He also finished the joints and spread mud as time allowed. Dancer danced around a brick job, keeping everything flowing like snow melting into a steaming hot spring. Yaotli would bring them deer jerky or elk tacos and ice-cold limeade. She loved to watch her son move and dance like a swift antelope, a sky full of shooting stars and lightning, or a striking rattlesnake.

When they finished a job, they moved on. After all the fine stonework on Inn of the Mountain Gods for the Mescalero Apache in southern New Mexico, they traveled south into Mexico. Dancer met a young lady called Valentina, so he stayed behind, and they camped in the mountains, near a hide out of Geronimo's. They ate peyote and caught rainbow trout. He soon got the urge to travel and transport. Dancer sadly said adios, it was understood. He helped Johnny, build a museum of stone near Running Water Draw, New Mexico. Dancer loved working with his father. He enjoyed the sun, wind, the pure act of creation, and most of all the camaraderie of the other working men. Johnny and Yaotli knew Dancer lived in two worlds. The world where he stood and more important, the world where his mind took him. He was an inventive genius, and his parents never stifled his experiments.

Dancer loved to take things apart and see what was inside and what made them tick. Nothing was off limits; watches, televisions, telephones, coffee pots, microwave ovens, cars, motorcycles, anything mechanical or digital was interesting. He improved plasma torches, brick saws, rifles, remote controls, motorized model airplanes, cellular phones, satellite dishes, and computers. Dancer made things smaller, faster, and better.

Dancer studied all ten dimensions and string theory. He developed a four-dimensional, ultraviolet infrared pigment siphoning extracting regurgitator. This was for tattoos and later for paintings. The FDUVIOPSER for short the

67

VIRPO, removed tattoos instantly with no pain. The regurgitator could duplicate the exact ink to anyone or thing, also painlessly. The invention could siphon pigments from any painting in the world and replicate the art, making the original a forgery and the new painting authentic.

He demonstrated his invention for his parents on his Uncle Woody that visited from Milwaukee. Woody had been a weapons master on ships and sailed all over the world. He had gotten tattoos on his entire body, something he deeply regretted. Dancer's Virpo Machine was the size of a toaster. Within minutes, his ink vanished, his family almost fainted and they screamed in pleasure. Dancer made sure Woody did not want any of his tattoos back on, then he poured the ink into a five-gallon bucket. Next, he pointed his Virpo at an ugly Elvis painting in velvet, he made it vanish, ten minutes later he returned the ink as it was.

Yaotli, Johnny, and Woody grew worried about Dancer's invention. They knew he would never have to work again, but if the Virpo Machine fell into the wrong hands, great damage and harm could be done. Dancer explained that he could make the invention work only on tattoo molecules. That way no one could forge paintings or money. He decided to patent the Virpo Machine and test the market for demand. He wanted to control making the factories where the machines would be assembled. Uncle Woody owned a gun shop, and they could expand it into a small factory. That would be a great diving board. There should be a big demand and plenty of money to be made. Statistics were that one in three people with tattoos regretted getting them. It was painful and expensive to have their ink removed with lasers or the abrasion method.

Dancer and Valentina would change the world, somewhat.

The Lowriders of El Paso del Norte

Looking around at all the famous
Beatniks, I wondered why I'd been
invited to read and the flyer had my name

On the main night of three, a big
shot asked me out of the blue to
start the gig, I realized an ulterior
motive to my invitation

I'd been watching this young drummer
in the back of a pickup entertaining two
young Cherry Valley ladies, I asked him
to beat the conga while I did my thing

We found a bigger louder drum and he
started jackhammering a rhythm, I started
with a coyote whoophowl from the back
of the room making the audience turn if
they wanted to see me dance Apache

I woke up everyone screaming "This is for
the lowriders in El Paso del Norte, now
let's fucking get down like Gumby"

Jumping on stage for the second poem, the
drum was beating that crowd into a frenzied
dervish, we had them in our palms and left
them all jonesing and wanting more

Later I wrote a poem about when
the Monkees asked Jimi Hendrix to
open for them and he started playing
with his teeth and set his guitar on fire.

Sky

A blue Lincoln sat in the driveway, behind Buffalo's van. Guitar and some type of wind instrument could be heard from out back. Buffalo was playing with a dark-haired beauty. She was blowing into a rondador from the Andes. Her notes had a serene and at the same time furious quality. They stopped long enough for introductions. Lucy said, "Please, don't let us interrupt you."

Sky was her name; quills of porcupine decorated her pure black hair. Her deep blue eyes shimmered in the morning sun. She played oblivious to Nicky or Lucy, when the song finished, her face took on aspects of a French vineyard and an Apache war maiden. Nicky finally felt love at first sight, it blossomed in his heart and attempted to overwhelm him. They strolled down to the stream, arm in arm. A golden eagle circled three times and landed in a nearby Joshua tree. Sky kissed him hard, he felt her tongue dart inside his mouth.

"You are the chosen one," Sky said. "You must go with me to the desert, where my ancestors once lived."

"Another lady told me the same thing this morning and gave me more money, than I ever dreamed of," replied Nicky.

"Money is only paper. I offer you an eternity in paradise," she answered.

They returned to the house. Lucy protested Nicky leaving. "Why don't you hang on to this check, until I get back," he said. Buffalo calmed Lucy's fears somewhat, by pulling her onto his lap. Of all the women, Nicky had known, Sky was by far the most enchanting and mysterious. She removed her shoes, jeans, and panties, explaining she wanted Nicky in the proper state of arousal, when they arrived at their destination. The road led down out of the mountains, but Nicky hardly noticed, he had a one-track mind.

"The place I am taking you is sacred ground. Geronimo would bring his warriors here to rest and heal themselves, after raiding into Mexico. We will eat peyote and you will have what you seek," she said.

Nicky kept thinking Geronimo's Mona Lisa. He painted Sky in his mind. Her skin was flowing honey, melon shaped breasts, a flat stomach, and a waterfall of cascading hair on her shoulders. An enigmatic smile suggested any wish would be fulfilled.

The dirt brown hills seemed to vibrate with a life of their own. The sand was warm and inviting. The peyote buttons crawled like fuzzy green caterpillars down Nicky's throat, threatening to choke him. Sky handed him tequila to wash them down. Nicky had never felt like this before. They undressed each other, feeling the rush and surge of the drug enhanced lust.

Kissing his way down her body, he reached her pubic triangle. He marveled at the blackness and orange stripes, it was so completely dark, it was void of color. The closer Nicky remained to Sky's pussy, the stronger became the force drawing him inside. It was a gentle soothing suction at first, but then he felt his tongue being pulled out of his face. The suction grew intense. He was slowly being swallowed, steadily disappearing inside her tiger pussy. His entire head was inside her and he couldn't breathe. Then he felt his body spinning, uncontrollably, until he was gone completely. The tiger whirlpool of life reclaimed him. Vanished and vanquished, Nicky was no more.

38 Flavors of Dog While Listening to Moby Grape

A semi-warped mind, 102 tears
of God, time is wiser than people,
dying is just going to sleep and
waking up on the other side

Stick a banana in your ear, play
with a warm slice of baloney,
the panther ate the rose, a delicious
morsel of ghost, memories, rain

Rivers, thunder. ravens' mellow jazz
composition, soothing, *Can I Walk
Down the Street Naked If I Want To,*
shine your red Carlos Santana stilettos.

Sweet Baby Jesus

Jesus was born a twelve-pound baby, on Route 66, almost killing his mother. His parents were proud of him, except for his size. He gobbled baby food like a starving goat. His mother tried to burp him, but he cut loose with some strong stinky loud farts. His father, Jesus Senior was a large construction worker, he laid bricks and could build just about anything. When his mom gave the baby to him, he patted him on the back and the stench damn near choked the old man. His dad started calling him Fart Baby. Sometimes appropriate nicknames stick for life. They would go grocery shopping and if anyone bothered them or was rude, they'd aim Fart Baby's little lethal ass at them, and he'd fire away like a cannon. Jesus Junior curled eyebrows, made strong men want to puke, made women scream, and made people scatter. His parents took Fart Baby to the doctor, he said he'll probably grow out of it. That never happened, he just got worse.

Confucius Blues

Plowing Boustrophedon behind a
Missouri mule from sunup to sun
down in an oneiric indigo daze

Schadenfreude of Plato, Kant,
Nietzsche, Buddha, Confucius,
Averroes, Schopenhauer, Spinoza

Ghost Dance warriors, united dead
and living, Sitting Bull knew how
to make war not love and love not war,
I feel a déjà vu annihilation coming.

Red Vineyards Near Arles

Was the only painting he sold while living,
in 1880 at age 27, he decided to become
an artist, he taught himself to draw and
paint, supported by his brother, Theo

He painted 2,000 works in 10 years at
a furious pace, 900 paintings and 1,100
drawings, he used impasto paint in thick
textures by brush, palette knife, and hands

In 1886 he joined Theo in Paris and met
Degas, Toulouse-Lautrec, Gauguin, and
Pissarro, he and Gauguin argued

Gauguin lopped off his ear with a sword
and cut curious zigzags above his ear,
they lied to the police saying he did it
to keep Gauguin out of prison, in June

1889, he went to Saint Remy-de-Provence
Asylum, where from his window facing

east just before sunrise he painted Starry
Night, his dying words were "the sadness
will last forever," his art will live forever.

Smell the Music

Louis Armstrong = Grapefruit

Miles Davis = Boiled Eggs

Jaco Pastorius = Biscuits

Prince = Strawberries

Johnny Cash = Black Licorice

Dolly Parton = Pecan Pie

Bob Marley = Bananas

Willie Nelson = Pine Cones

Janis Joplin = Southern Comfort

Jimi Hendrix = Marijuana

Elvis Presley = Bacon

B.B. King = Cigars

Nina Simone = Coffee

Pearl Bailey = Iced Tea

Taylor Swift = Bubble Gum

Tina Turner = Cherries

Mick Jagger = Pizza

John Lennon = Oranges

Joni Mitchell = Cigarettes

Tom Waits = Beer

Carlos Santana = Cinnamon.

Mastodon Kush

Johnny dreamed about, one-eyed Juanita raising mastodons near the grassy hills of Clovis. He was glad his cousin Dancer was visiting; he wrote down ideas. Dancer's family were storytellers. They could whoop a yarn like pink cotton candy at the Santa Fe fair. Dancer was the dreamcatcher in the sun or moon light. He attempted to string words together, as poems or stories or songs. His parents drank rattlesnake venom, snorted devil's breath, and read to him about Houdini while he was a baby. Dancer was different. Him and Johnny went outside to try some wicked fucking weed. Johnny was listening to 5 Seconds of Summer. The weed was tight gummy buds interwoven with purple glowing Kush threads, washed down with tiswin. They looked up and saw seven raccoons in the cherry tree, lit up by a comet zinging across the champagne electric blue Van Gogh heavens. Port told Johnny about his latest adventure in the Jemez Mountains. He built a retaining wall for a medical clinic and helped a man with his foundation and fireplace. He met a Korean lady with all her fingers and her thumbs shortened by one digit. It got cold and Port told her it was a four-dog night.

She got mad thinking he called her a dog. She said dogs are good eating too. The honeymoon hit the fan. He couldn't help looking at those nubby fingers.

Johnny laughed his ass off. By morning Dancer had vanished into the antelope mirage distance.

Coozeman

*"There ain't no jackoff compared to that wonder-hole." Charles
Bukowski*

Dancer never thought he'd be selling wigs to soul sisters,
but life throws lots knuckle balls and rocks. The Korean
folks he worked for were good people, but didn't have the
gift for gab, plus they loved to eat garlic. Their breath could
make your eyes water and skid stains in your undies. After
the lady dropped a 45 on the floor on Dancer's second day
of work, he kept his eyes wide open. She came back awhile
later and bought a wig and an extension from Dancer, it
happened to be the day he started getting paid on
commission. It was a nice score, the lady asked him if he
needed a piece. Dancer said always, she meant her semi-
automatic. Dancer said he'd take both. He waited until the
Koreans went to lunch and took her in the backroom and
ravaged her. Dancer ate that pussy then fucked her like Big
Leroy breaking in a punk in Alcatraz. There was no
tomorrow, yesterday, or future, only a sex machine gone
haywire. That black woman screamed, "Bloody fucking
murder, fire, rape, son of a bitch, you're the devil, you

white motherfucker. The way you do sex is a dirty sin." She gave him the 45 and left before his bosses got back, she came back a week later with a friend, they asked Dancer about some hair and a piece. "What do you have in mind ladies?" "Can you handle us both? We have a 357 magnum and a 9-millimeter." "Let's get a room nearby." They climbed into their Lincoln and cruised to liquor store for some libations. On the television was a fat chick telling Dr. Phil she'd lost one hundred pounds in one week. He told her she must've been cutting off body parts. Things got funky freaky fast. After a couple of hours, they were both sauced and snoring. Dancer wrapped his new shooting irons in a towel and got the plastic bag from the bathroom trashcan. He stopped in a bar on the way home and saw a ferret chained to a pool table. He asked what they fed it; a lady said the poor thing only eats Captain Crunch cereal. Dancer bought the ferret for twenty dollars, he had no idea what to do with it. Maybe he could teach it to eat snatch.

Tilt

On the lam from a marijuana beef, the state north seemed more favorable to my predicament and behavior. Radical. Outrageous. Entirely without redemption or qualm.

The old Argonaut Hotel in Denver sat empty, semi-condemned across from Argonaut Liquor on Colfax Avenue. Every wino, bum, hippie, hobo, hooker, and hustler scored booze there.

Promising the landlord to fix up his building, we started the first in-town commune. As one of the founding members and most lucrative pussy getting smokable drug dealer, it's appropriate that I relate the following events surrounding my inhabitation of the above-mentioned den of inequity and the catastrophic calamity.

I would ask you to let me remain in the shadows, as the statutes of limitations have expired on most of my supposedly criminal acts. Especially since many of our past politicians have smoked dope. So, I'm not considered such an outlaw anymore.

There were many drugs used there. Orange sunshine, blue cheer, purple microdot, blotter, chocolate mescaline, magic mushrooms, and peyote: all doorways to madness gladness sadness. Skeletons dancing from closets, Timothy Leary's ghost, Jerry Garcia grateful and dead. Save the ladybug. Talk to plants. Pet rocks. Free love. Jail hate. Blow jobs. Tuna fish. Smoke morning glory. Climb trees. Fuck pigs. Save green stamps.

Life/Death. Papa's little squirt. Yo mama's titty. Uncle Sam's penis. Worm food. In that order.
California falls into the Pacific. Hollywood is Atlantis. Calling Aquaman. Saguaros surfing with Joshua trees. Arizona beaches. The world is a small turd circling a ball of fire. Lucifer is drinking Mad Dog and playing God's pinball machine.

COVID

If you don't want
the vaccine or want
to wear a mask.

Go cut the seatbelts
from your car and
disable your airbags.

John Deere Doesn't Play

The man got tired of mowing his huge lot with a push mower and went and bought a fancy riding machine. He jumped on it and did some doughnuts and ran it top end and showed off to his neighbors. Later he went inside for lemonade and then went to mow his entire lawn. There was a fairly steep hill on the side of his house, and he roared into it. The mower flipped several times with him under the deck. The newly sharpened blade cut off his penis and mutilated his groin area. A passerby heard his screams and called an ambulance. The medics applied pressure and put his bloody sex organ in a container of ice. The doctors attached his penis to an artery in his arm, to keep blood flowing into it until they could do reconstructive surgery. Reporters came and wrote about his predicament and people made cruel jokes. His wife was unhappy and left him. He finally disappeared. Last time he was seen, he was fishing off a jetty in Lake Michigan.

The Sky Was Larger Than Los Angeles and New York City Having Mad Sex

Angelinos with tattoos made of cocaine,
you could snort right off and watch
the skin change until the next time
they wanted to be a human billboard

Having invented the Magic Straw, I was
richer than Hitler, I bought a crib in the
Pecan Mountains and became a master of
disguise, I was a chameleon of accents

I used the funky names like Fink and Dipstick
and many more unsavory handles, my cook
was missing her thumb, I wondered if I ate it,
I looked up at the blue night and played mandolin

Deciding to give my money to homeless vets,
Native Americans, and the needy, I would ask
them to buy and cremate Mount Rushmore and
turn it into a vast vegetable garden and orchard.

A Ninja with a Boner

She loved me because of poetry
I am wood, you are fire
I am the beach, you are the ocean

When you're in my arms, nothing is wrong
I'm lying on magic clouds, waiting for you
my love is clinging to the cliff

"My dog ate 7 cockroaches, do
you think it will get sick?"

"Naw, I used to eat them
on tortillas down in Mexico"

Six mailboxes, a coyote, and a ninja
with a hard on, Hercules, Copernicus
the fear of God and love of Lucifer.

Kingfish and the VA Ordeal

My ordeal became a bit nasty. The lab, even the cold dye Cat scan was okay. The plastic surgeon was an a-hole with a capital A. He disrespected me and was real rude, he told me to come back in 2 weeks, I said no. He said what do you mean no? I told him I am 68 years old, a Honorable Discharge, I am a trained killing machine, unafraid of jail or death. I would prefer to see another doctor because if you smart mouth me ever again, I might break you up. This happened yesterday, the VA called for me to return in 13 days. I guess I have no choice. From my scan they found small gall stones, colon diverticulitis, and my aorta aneurysm, nothing to be done about any of it, yet. Luckily, I don't have ulcers. This happened yesterday, the VA called for me to return in 13 days. I guess I have no choice. It just hit midnight and this letter got my fingers warmed up and I'm listening to Kingfish Ingram. (a 22-year-old fat Southern black blues lad, he'd give Jimi a run for his money)

Magdalena

Scarfing vagabond goulash
from Mexican sombrero
hub caps stolen from a
turquoise low rider short
in the valley of Albuquerque

Spanish dagger roots, flowers,
stems, and blanco corn tortillas
prickly pear tuna, serrano, pob-
lano, Copper Canyon sotol

Slow your cinnamon roll, mama
cooch, no need to gank the skank
let's booty call tango fandango

Roots of the desert dagger are
full of saponins, a toxin that can
be used to stun fish without injury.

Mexican Jumping Beans

Gave her an eighteen-year-old
rattlesnake tail button glued
to a popsicle stick, she told me

To kiss her pussy, I was fourteen
and she was seventeen and a
distant cousin, she'd already

Caught me jerking off while watching
her and her friends showering
after swimming in her pool.

27 Hammerheads Circled Ever Closer

Six mailboxes of rejects, a geisha
with crotch-less panties in a blue
silk stork robe, Confucius love,
the fear of God and love of sin

Don Quixote eating peyote, while
wolves, grizzlies, Tasmanian devils,
and cat-sized mosquitoes try to
drain your blood in murderous rage

She never knew I was a legerdemain
charlatan holding hands with magic,
27 hammerheads circled ever closer.

Birdman from Albuquerque

Granted, the pigeons were annoying
but not to the degree my lady and
neighbors took it, they were livid
paralyzed by bird anger, pure hatred
pigeon shit rolled onto the sidewalk
and porch, grayish white curls and
globs, the birds could be heard cooing
flapping, and fornicating, laying eggs
and pecking gravel off all the shingles
they suggested a machinegun, shotgun
at least a flamethrower, I thought this
rather drastic, I bought a plastic hoot
owl with an attached rope you pulled
to make its wings flutter, I felt like the
hunchback of Notre Dame pulling that
rope, the pigeons shit on the owl and
me and laughed, I bought a mean looking
rubber snake and got a raptor bird call,
it sounded like a sick duck, they played
tug of war with the snake and had fun,

I tried rags soaked in vinegar and Clorox

they fashioned luxury nests, then I heard

of a product called Roost, a gooey sap

you smeared on the roof, it was supposed

to be just sticky enough when the birds

landed and felt trapped, they would stay

away, I tried it, they roosted all right, but

it was permanent, now my roof was covered

with dead pigeons in various states of decay,

vultures and other carrion birds are swooping

in for tidbits, the bird watcher's society burned

my figure in effigy, some witch doctors are

poking voodoo dolls of me and my pain is

excruciating, I suspect now I am ready for

the flamethrower or even a bazooka.

Copping Some Crack

Two soul brothers stopped off
in Philadelphia on their way home
from a big march in Washington D. C.

"The city of brotherly love, my
black ass, whitey don't love us any
more here than he does in the capitol,
we drive all that way and the president
ain't even there, fuck America"

"Pass me some of that Tokay, it has an
excellent bouquet, you should not be
so hard on Uncle Sambo, we might
get a black man in office someday"

"Whitey brought us here in chains,
he's gonna keep us locked or glocked,
40 acres and a mule, my black ass"

"You got that right bro, that's why
it's called the White House, it's for
the white man if a black got in there,
you think they'd change the name?"

They pulled over and finished the bottle
and opened a fresh bajow, "See that
flag, I'm gonna burn it after I take a
shit and wipe my ass, then I'm gonna
piss all over the Liberty Bell"

The black cat lowered his pants and
dropped a load, he managed to wipe
himself, but he burned his fingers
trying to get the flag ignited

He started pissing on the bell, his pal
was so drunk he staggered into him
he yelled, "Hey motherfucker, my dick
is stuck in the crack, somebody HELP"

Two cops came running with drawn
guns, "We'll help" "Do you want to
shoot it off, or can I?"

A Peanut Butter Sandwich

After being her patient for ten years, my regular medical doctor finally did a rear end exam on me. I was older than her and she was incredibly beautiful, I felt kind of strange with my pants down and her finger up my butt. It was almost erotic, but not quite. She found a hemorrhoid and asked if I wanted her to cut it off after she froze it, I declined. She said she would refer me to a proctologist. I looked up what a proctologist was, and the medical definition was they dealt with disorders of the colon, rectum, and anus. I always thought the rectum was an anus.

The day of my appointment I felt nervous my sphincter wouldn't cooperate. I wanted to defecate well and then take a shower to get baby butt clean. I walked into the doctor's office and this young man sat there with a smirk on his face and three females all in white coats.

"Please go behind the curtain and remove everything from the waist down and put on a paper gown," he said. "Now bend over the table as far as possible." They rolled a spotlight over next to my ass, it felt like I was going to be interrogated by the Gestapo.

"Now this might be uncomfortable." I felt eight hands, with blue squeaky rubber gloves pulling my butt cheeks apart. They were speaking to each other, ignoring me completely. Then they put the lubricant gel all over my rectum or maybe it was my anus. They each took turns finger fucking me and shoving flashlights up my keister. "See, now that wasn't so bad, was it." He slapped me on the rump and handed me one tissue to mop up all the damage they'd done. The women sat there grinning as I made a feeble attempt to sop up all their mess. "By the way, we need to schedule a follow up visit."

I waddled out of there, feeling like my mechanic had given me a lube job and went crazy with his grease gun. I called my personal doctor and asked if it was absolutely necessary to return to the four proctologists from hell. All she said was yes, with a touch of humor in her voice.

Sometimes I get brilliant ideas that are bizarre. Before my next visit I got two jars of crunchy peanut butter and a container of non-toxic paste glue. I mixed this combination all up in a huge mixing bowl and let it set up

101

somewhat. I got in front of my lady's big full-length mirror with a big batter knife, and I spackled my asshole, really packing it in and slathered my upper thighs. I put a loaf of bread in my backpack and headed off to the doctor's office. When I went behind the curtain to undress, the bizarre concoction felt like dried shit. It was difficult to walk and keep a straight face. I carried my pack with the bread and a spreading knife.

When I bent over the examining table, there was utter silence. I started laughing, I took the knife and bread and scraped off some fake shit and made a sandwich. I took a huge bite and asked if anyone would care for lunch. Four heads were wagging in unison horizontally in a negatory reply. Getting dressed I split. Calling up my doctor when I arrived home, I asked if any further appointments would be required with the anus examiner. She replied, "No and never invite me to lunch."

Under the Atlantic

A British man with a name I had never heard sent poems to a blog site I jointly run. He said he was in Spain caring for a sick dog, I had an eerie feeling something supernatural was happening. His girlfriend was trying to help him to return to England. He figured he would crash with his parents, work as a gardener, and write. I called him and said I was on my way to Paris for a reading and to meet a French publisher that accepted my sex novella. The Frenchman said he tried reading it on the bus, but he kept getting a hard on. My pal said in England they call it an erection on, also the American's use of the word cunt was frowned upon. I finished the marijuana joint I was smoking and wrote him and said, "Cunt and hard on is bad?" He just laughed as I hung up.

After taking several Xanax and slurping martinis I killed my panic about flying. I saw the Eiffel Tower from a taxi, but I was still very fucked up on the way to my hotel. I did my reading at The Shakespeare and Co. Bookstore; I sold a few chapbooks and talked a bit of smack. My pal was sitting there grinning. I did not know it was him until he introduced himself. He told me the dog died and he had buried it in his friend's backyard, but something had dug it up in the night. He suggested taking the Chunnel train to London before I was to head back to America, I agreed.

We had a few beers and smoked a blunt of hash mixed with tobacco before boarding the train. It was a two-hour trip by high-speed rail. We were an hour under the water when the train stopped, and all the lights went out. I felt anxiety crawling up the back of my throat like a caterpillar with gonorrhea, especially when I saw my British pal being attacked by a red eyed demon zombie dog from Spain. I took off my shoe started beating on the canine and screamed a Mexican Indian cure chant. It must have had some effect, the lights flickered, and the dog vanished.

I ordered a bottle of gin and poured my pal a few stiff drinks. We were both tanked by the time we hit Great Britain, but at least we were still breathing. Spanish dog zombies are sure as fuck not man's best friend.

It Has Been a Minute

My cousin, Traci knew I was bumming around New Mexico and Mexico after the army. She left a message for me, saying there was plenty of work in Milwaukee. I had been there a few times and liked it, except the length of winter. Having spent a few years in Germany and the mountains, I was used to freezing weather.

I got a job at Briggs and Stratton, working second shift in the small crankshaft department. I was making big money, but I disliked it. I won a ten-thousand-dollar check pool and scored on the finest lady in the factory, that owned a Corvette. I lasted two months and flew back to Albuquerque. I bought a Buick for ten dollars and tuned it up and loaded it with mota and headed north. I got job across the street from my cousin, at a tavern. The place looked like a cantina from a John Wayne movie. After I broke up a few fights I was made assistant manager. I met the three Palicios brothers, Armando, Anselmo, and Ishmael. Anselmo worked with Traci in a Mexican café, he was known as Sam. Ishmael was known as Joe. Armando was Mando. They all three thought they could shoot pool,

I taught them to play snooker, then they really learned how to win money on bar pool table. We bowled; they waxed my ass.

Then we started fishing. Mando and I bought a wooden boat, which needed lots of work. We fixed it up and hit all the inner lakes, mostly avoiding Lake Michigan, it was like an ocean with huge waves. We fished rivers and streams catching all kinds of fish. We got a bunch of guys to chip in and took two charter boat trips on the big lake. We landed salmon, lake trout, and rainbows. We took them to a guy with a meat shop and he smoked them, that was some tasty fish.

There was a jetty made of concrete chunks that extended about a hundred yards out into Lake Michigan. It was under the Hoan Bridge, also known as the Bridge to Nowhere. The Blues Brothers filmed their famous car jump on it. All three brothers and I would fish and party on the jetty when the waves were not too fierce. For bait, we tried nightcrawlers, grub worms, wax worms, minnows, corn, artificial baits, Rapalas, spoons. We got skunked every day and night.

One old man caught his limit in trout and salmon every time we walked past him. I tried to speak to him, but he was not friendly. I noticed; he was drinking Olde English

800 a malt liquor made by Miller Brewery in Milwaukee. I considered it horse piss with a kick. I went and bought two six packs, I made my special Guatemalan Coffee Huehuetenango Zaculeu and filled my thermos. When I got to the lake front, Mando saw the beer and said, "I thought you were on the wagon?" "Watch and learn."

We stopped at the old man. "We brought you some beer. Maybe you could give us a few lessons?" The old man laughed. He handed me a cold one, I gave it to Mando. "I ate some Mexican jumping beans last night and have been shitting like Hannibal's elephant." Mando looked at the malt liquor like it was canned nastiness. He popped the top and started chugging.

"Catching the bait is the main trick. The bait is small smelt, not too small, or too large. You must use a dip net with a long extending rod. This is extremely critical, never touch the smelt with your fingers because each tiny fish has silvery sides. You must get tweezers used in stamp collecting, they are flattened and wide at the tips. You slip the smelt onto a small snelled hook. You use a slip bobber with a lead shot weight. You put one line shallow and the other deep. To locate where the fish are feeding. Wait fifteen minutes for a bite, readjust the depths If you have no luck."

They drank beer, I drank my Guatemalan Coffee Huehuetenango Zaculeu. We caught so many fish after that lesson. It was too damn easy.

I'd Rather Be an Elephant

There will be a few good moments, but mostly it will get worse. Cars and loved ones dying. Yesterday after 2 years of dental work to get perfect teeth for a 68-year-old "rode hard- and put-up wet catfish", they started doing a root canal, which ended up being an extraction. My 3 fake teeth and wisdom tooth extraction all for nothing except for a shit load of money. My lady thought I'd died, they brought her back where I was, 1 dental student, 3 professors, 4 asst. all working me over. My wife thinking WTF! Since Thanksgiving 6 poet pals died, family gone. The small press will always be a war, out of 10 new people you meet 3 might end up being amigo/as. When I get tiny royalty checks, $.42 or $2.11 my wife gets ticked off because she likes to balance to the penny or peso. Hang tough, you have your youth, when you come to the fork in the road, take it.

Catfish McDaris' most infamous chapbook is *Prying* with Jack Micheline and Charles Bukowski. His best readings were in Paris at the Shakespeare and Co. Bookstore and with Jimmy "the Ghost of Hendrix" Spencer in NYC on 42nd St. He's done over 25 chaps in the last 30 years. He's been in the *New York Quarterly*, *Slipstream*, *Pearl*, *Main St. Rag*, *Café Review*, *Chiron Review*, *Zen Tattoo*, *Wormwood Review*, *Great Weather For Media*, *Silver Birch Press*, and *Graffiti* and been nominated for 15 Pushcarts, Best of Net in 2010, 2013, and 2014, he won the Uprising Award in 1999, and won the Flash Fiction Contest judged by the U.S. Poet Laureate in 2009. He was in the *Louisiana Review*, *George Mason Univ. Press*, and *New Coin* from Rhodes Univ. in South Africa. He's recently been translated into Spanish, French, Polish, Swedish, Arabic, Bengali, Mandarin, Yoruba, Tagalog, and Esperanto. His 30 years of published material is in the Special Archives Collection at Marquette Univ. in Milwaukee, Wisconsin. Catfish McDaris won the Thelonious Monk Award in 2015. He's a 3-year Army artillery veteran, from Albuquerque and Milwaukee. Bukowski's Indian pal Dave Reeve, editor of Zen Tattoo gave Catfish McDaris his name when he, (Steven) spoke of wanting to quit the post office and start a catfish farm. After the army, he spent a summer shark fishing in the Sea of Cortez, built adobe houses, tamed wild horses around the Grand Canyon, worked in a zinc smelter in the panhandle of Texas, and painted flag poles in the wind. He ended at the post office in Milwaukee.

Made in the USA
Middletown, DE
08 November 2021

51724288R00066